This space is for your
favourite among the
photographs you took
on August 14th

August 14th 1987
MY DAY FOR LIFE

ONE DAY FOR LIFE

Photographs by the people of Britain, taken on a single day

With a foreword by
HRH The Duchess of York

SEARCH 88

BANTAM PRESS

London · New York · Toronto · Sydney · Auckland

TRANSWORLD PUBLISHERS LTD
61 – 63 Uxbridge Road, London W5 5SA

TRANSWORLD PUBLISHERS (AUSTRALIA) PTY LTD
15 – 23 Helles Avenue, Moorebank NSW 2170

TRANSWORLD PUBLISHERS (NZ) LTD
Cnr Moselle and Waipareira Aves,
Henderson, Auckland

Published 1987 by Bantam Press,
a division of Transworld Publishers Ltd
Copyright © SEARCH 88 Ltd 1987
Designed by A.D. Consultants, London
Typeset by Lazy Dog, London
Printed in West Germany by
Mohndruck Graphische Betriebe GmbH, Gütersloh

British Library Cataloguing in Publication Data

One day for life: photographs by the people
of Britain, taken on a single day.
1. Photography, Artistic
779'.0942   TR654

ISBN 0-593-01464-2

Contents

HRH The Duchess of York
CRATHIE CHURCH
Balmoral, Scotland

On August 14th, 1987, an ordinary day became quite extraordinary when thousands of people all over the country celebrated their existence and captured it on film; including myself.

This book records what the people of Britain did that day and the photographs in it are remarkable for their quality and for the way they show that Britain, seen through the eyes of different people, is a country of both character and beauty.

It is also a country that is touched by tragedy – the tragedy that cancer brings to sufferers and their families. This book is for those who are still fighting, to thank them for their inspiration and for those who, in the end, we couldn't help, to thank them for their courage. It is also for the doctors, scientists, nurses and volunteers who care for them and lastly, it is for all of us – because there are few of us whose lives have not been touched in some way by cancer.

Sarah,

HRH The DUCHESS of YORK

HRH Prince Andrew

Our grateful thanks to our four major sponsors, without whom
this book would not exist.

The Judges

Chris Coles, ADP

Standing left to right: Patrick Lichfield; Jane Bown; Richard Young (judging panel co-ordinator); Terence Donovan; Dick Jones; Gene Nocon (judging panel co-ordinator); Terry O'Neill; George Hughes; Sue Davies; Gareth Pyne-James (founder and project director of SEARCH 88). Seated left to right: Linda McCartney; Don McCullin; Heather Angel

We would like to thank the people whose task it was to select the photographs that make up this book. These include members of photographic societies and clubs throughout the country who very kindly gave up their weekends to do the initial sorting.

Also, our grateful thanks go to the team of highly professional photographic judges who had the difficult task of choosing the final 350 pictures for this book. They were:

HEATHER ANGEL
JANE BOWN
SUE DAVIES
TERENCE DONOVAN
GEORGE HUGHES
DICK JONES
PATRICK LICHFIELD
LINDA McCARTNEY
DON McCULLIN
TERRY O'NEILL

The
EARLY
HOURS

12.00-6.00

Just after midnight – the bright lights and music are over until the next show
begins. I wanted to capture on camera a quiet scene in London, an alternative
to my usual habitat of bustling theatreland. However, with the aeroplane
overhead and a passing boat on the river it too seemed busy and not so
very different after all. I knew I was not the only one on the way home in
the early morning.

DIANA RIGG

E. Aldred
GOOD MORNING, BRITAIN
1.15am: Central London

Mr I. Reynolds
A NEW DAWN
5.20am: Windsor, Berkshire

Stefan Morris
SWEET DREAMS?
5.50am: Maida Vale, London

Tony Simmester
EARLY MORNING, THE SHAMBLES
2.30am: The Shambles, York

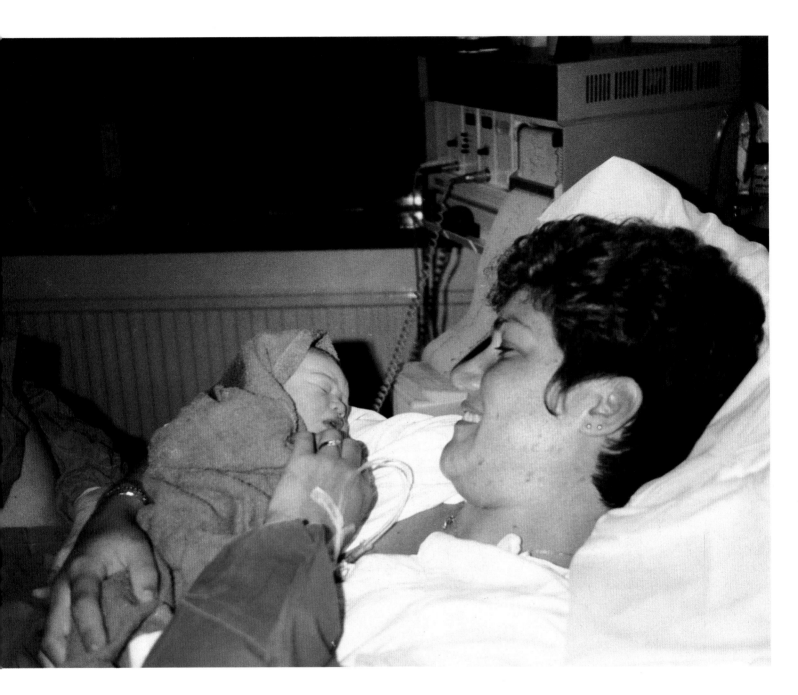

Lesley Copland
THE BIRTH OF EMMA, 3.57am
3.59am: Irvine, Ayrshire

John Maughan
DAWN – SHIP GOING TO SEA
5.15am: Tynemouth, Tyne & Wear

Christopher James
GIRL CRAZY
5.30am: Stoke-on-Trent

David M. Falconer
BRIDGES AT DAWN
5.30am: Newcastle Upon Tyne

P.L. Hill
TRANQUIL DAWN
5.30am: Dartmoor National Park

Overleaf:
Mr I. Reynolds
WINDSOR GREAT PARK – SUNRISE
5.30am: Windsor, Berkshire

Vivienne Smith
STORM AHEAD
5.50am: Poynton, Cheshire
Daily Express Winner

Gerald James Pecover
MORNING MIST
5.30am: White Hill, Kingsclere

David Brook
DEW ON SPIDER'S WEB
5.45am: Pevensey, East Sussex

Mr G.A. Targett
MORNING HAS BROKEN
5.55am: Putney, London

Denise Smith
OLIVER AND HIS DAD
5.50am: Buckingham

Mr I.R. Flaherty
SUNRISE OVER INDUSTRIAL
THAMES
6.00am: Greenwich, London

Tim Broad
CRAB FISHERMEN –
POOLE HARBOUR
6.00am: Poole Harbour, Dorset

Barry Snelgrove
BILLINGSGATE FISH MARKET
6.00am: Billingsgate, London

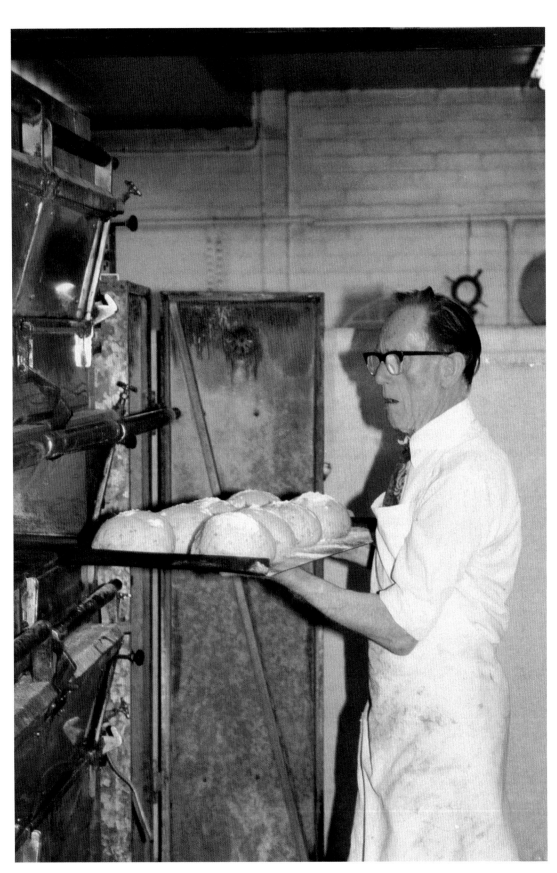

Colin Baker
EARLY MORNING GRANARY
6.00am: Marlow, Buckinghamshire

This picture suggests a subtle blend of nostalgia and challenge, with the former
encapsulated by the Perthshire hills and the latter represented by Gleneagles'
superb putting surfaces. It evokes memories of happy but moist summers in
Scotland, but also a realisation that I shall never, ever become a real golfer.
But hope springs eternal. The sun might shine and I might sink that long putt.
And if neither happens, there is always the prospect of a 'dram' to breathe
warmth back into the soul.

DENYS HENDERSON

The
MORNING

6.00-10.00

One of the most enjoyable sights for me is to look out upon my yard in the early
morning to see the expectant faces of the horses in training, whilst everything
is still peaceful... before another busy day. The reason I photographed these two
horses above, Aberoy and Turn Blue, was because they seemed to be in deep
discussion, whether it was concerning the weather, their next meal or even
something as important as the next race... I don't know. Horses are my life,
I would feel so empty without them; this is why I chose this photograph as my
contribution for *One Day for Life*. Whilst I was ill the one goal that kept me going
was my hope and determination to ride Aldaniti and win the
Grand National.

BOB CHAMPION

Margaret Hutcherson
(FRED AND MAUDE)
JUST GOOD FRIENDS
6.45am: Trowbridge, Wiltshire

Joyce M. Willson
EARLY-MORNING DELIVERY
7.10am: Boston, Lincolnshire

Pauline McCulloch
BUBBLE TROUBLE
6.30am: Brentwood, Essex

Jacqueline Lamberty
HOT AIR FLIERS
6.30am: Bristol, Avon

Joyce M. Willson
WALKING THE DOG
6.45am: Boston, Lincolnshire

Chris Scrivener
TIME FOR A QUICK NAP
8.00am: Spitalfields Market, London

Neil Fagan
THE EARLY MORNING RUSH
7.00am: King's Cross/
St Pancras Station

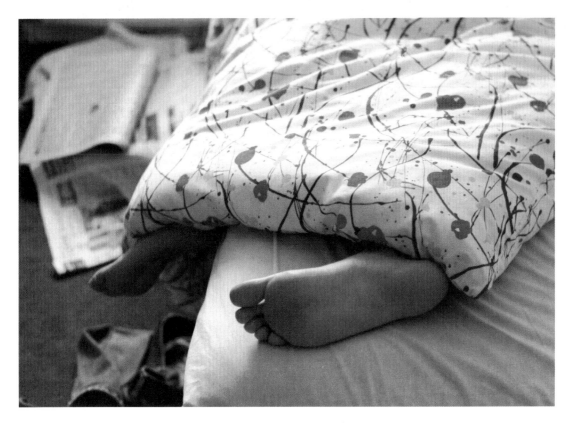

J. Peatling
ANDREW
7.00am: Bridgend, Mid Glamorgan

Harry Smith
LANDING THE COCKLE HARVEST
6.50am: Old Leigh, Essex

Peter Spalding
EARLY START
7.00am: Southwold, Suffolk

Elizabeth Stevens
MORNING EXERCISE, NORTH
COTSWOLD HUNT
7.20am: Snowshill, Gloucestershire

Clive B. Harrison
PAN PIPE BUSKER
7.30am: Bath, Avon

Mr W.W. Banner
ANOTHER DAY FOR LIVING
7.30am: Broadstairs, Kent

Trevor Brown
MORNING MIST OVER PEWSEY VALE
8.00am: Pewsey, Wiltshire

Patricia A. Buck
EARLY MORNING BALLOONS
IN BRISTOL
7.30am: Bristol, Avon

Marina MacLeod
PEACE OF CHELSEA
8.00am: Chelsea Embankment,
London

Mrs P. Passenger
EARLY MORNING PEACE
8.00am: Stevenage Lakes,
Hertfordshire

Glyn Elms
THE NEW BROOM
8.00am: Witney, Oxfordshire

Janet Patmore
HECTOR EATING BREAKFAST
(3rd HELPING!)
7.30am: Wokingham, Berkshire

David A. Holmes
PREPARATION, KELLOGGS
CYCLE RACE
8.15am: City Centre, Manchester

Mrs J. Wilkinson
GETTING A LIFT FROM LIFE
8.15am: Lichfield, Staffordshire

50

Paul Dawson
THE WORKING DAY'S EARLY START
8.30am: Royal Academy, Piccadilly

J.B. Whitby
RAY
8.30am: Abbey Park, Leicester

J.B. Whitby
BY THE RIVER SOAR
8.30am: Abbey Park, Leicester

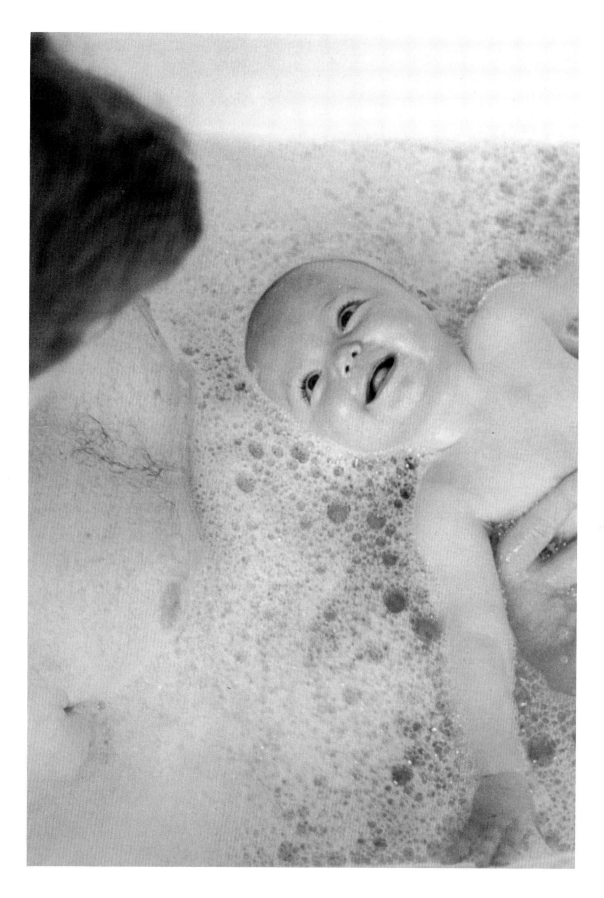

Jennifer Beeston
BATH WITH DADDY BEFORE
HE GOES TO WORK
8.30am: Clapham, London

Bill Clarke
BOY AND HIS DOG
8.30am: Hove Beach, Sussex

R.L.D. Cooper
IS THERE ANY FOR HIM?
8.30am: Gorgie Road, Edinburgh

Dorothy Antoinette Bennett
NECESSARY FOR LIFE
8.30am: Crewe, Cheshire

Roy Dodsworth
ALFRED'S BIRTHDAY
8.40am: Bradford, Yorkshire

Andrew Barden
HOLIDAYMAKERS PUSH
THE BOAT OUT
8.45am: North Landing,
Flamborough

Robert Stephen Wilkins
STAFF, ENVIRONMENTAL HEALTH
DEPT, CARDIFF
9.30am: Caerwys House, Cardiff

Ian Duncalf
THE FACE OF COMMUTING
8.55am: Farringdon Station, London

Mr P.J. Bunting
ANOTHER BEAUTIFUL DAY
TO BE ALIVE
9.00am: Ashover, Derbyshire

Mrs M.J. Somerville
WOMEN'S INSTITUTE MARKET
9.00am: Burford, Oxfordshire

John A. Plowman
THE DAILY ROUND
9.00am: West Coker, Somerset

Penny Stanley
MILK DELIVERY IN CLOVELLY
9.00am: Clovelly, Devon

Michael Griffiths
ERIC DE-SHIVING A DRAUGHT CASK
9.00am: Burton-on-Trent

Clive B. Harrison
LAST OFF THE TRAIN
9.15am: Bath, Avon

Ione Holbourne
FUNERAL OF SHIRLEY,
CANCER VICTIM
9.15am: Morriston Crematorium,
South Wales

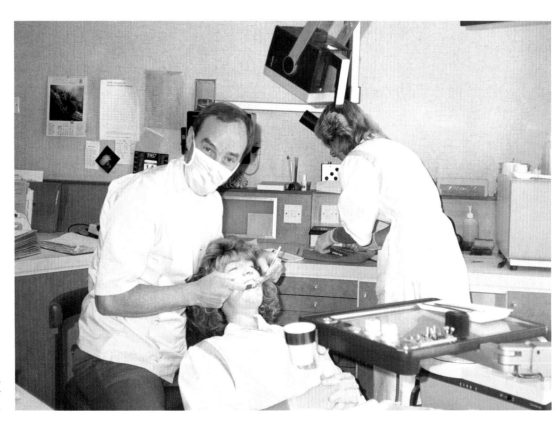

Miss E.B.C. Collins
KEN, MY FRIENDLY DENTIST
9.15am: Boscombe, Bournemouth

Opposite:
David Davenport
UP AND OVER
9.30am: Southend-on-Sea, Essex

Barry Day
HMS WARRIOR AND
VISITING JAPANESE SAILORS
10.00am: Portsmouth, Hampshire

T. Sinclair
TRAMP LOOKING INTO
BROADCASTING HOUSE
10.00am: Portland Place, London

Darrin King
FOUNTAIN,
ST GEORGE'S WAY GARDENS
10.00am: Stevenage, Hertfordshire

Mrs P.H.P. Adams
MY HUSBAND, THE GARDENER
10.00am: Old Catton, Norfolk

Mike Rose
THE 'TERRIBLE TWINS'
FANCY DRESS
10.00am: Ingatestone Play
Scheme, Essex

Gordon Gill
MEAT DELIVERY
10.00am: Westbury-on-Trym, Bristol

Rosemary Glenys Thomas
MODERN MISS, WALKMAN
AND GRAFFITI
10.00am: War Memorial Park,
Coventry

Mrs E.M. Haith
SCRUBBING THE BACK STEP
10.00am: Bradley Manor, Grimsby

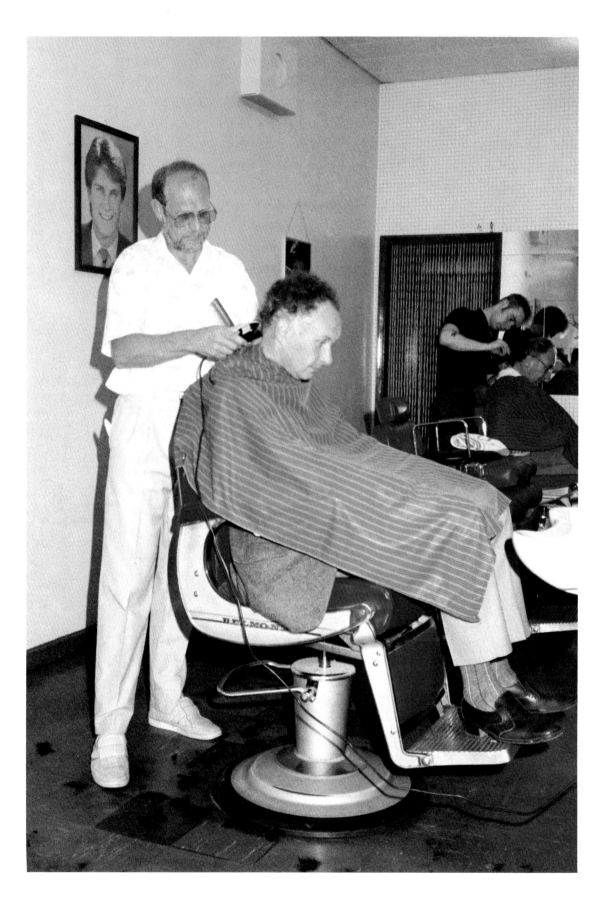

Harold W. Wheeler
STILL LIFE?
9.40am: St Albans, Hertfordshire

Rosanne Moss
WHEN DADDY GOES TO WORK
8.15am: Royston, Hertfordshire

Ian Trewren Thomas
BARREL ORGAN PHIL
9.30am: City Centre, Chester

Every year thousands of people from all over the world visit Knowle House in
Kent, the historic home of Lord Sackville. If I could, I would spend part of
every day in the magnificent parkland at Knowle – how lucky I am to have it so
close by. I'm forever struck by the tranquillity and beauty of the lush rolling
countryside – here the frustrations of daily battling with London traffic
disappear, problems cease to be so important, and one's feeling of well-being
improves. No wonder Knowle is where I chose to be during *One Day for Life*.

GLORIA HUNNIFORD

The
MIDDLE
of the DAY

10.00-2.00

This view across the lake has been an inspiration to me, not least in providing a
subject for my painting. Well, we call it a lake, but it is actually man-made,
constructed in 1806 to provide the nearby lead-smelting works with water.
On just such a morning as that on August 14th, I had come to view the house
we have now lived in for the past six years. My first glimpse of the lake not only
decided me to buy the house, but later most assuredly sowed the seeds in my
mind for my novel, *A Dinner of Herbs*.

CATHERINE COOKSON

Val Fiddaman
FUN ON THE FOURTEENTH
10.15am: Hunstanton, Norfolk

Kathleen M. Clarke
WAITING TO SERVE
10.09am: Cromer, Norfolk

Brian Dalton
PAINTING FOR PLEASURE
10.12am: Hessle, North Humberside

Geoffrey Deith
EXPERT GUILDER AT WORK
10.30am: Stoke-on-Trent,
Staffordshire

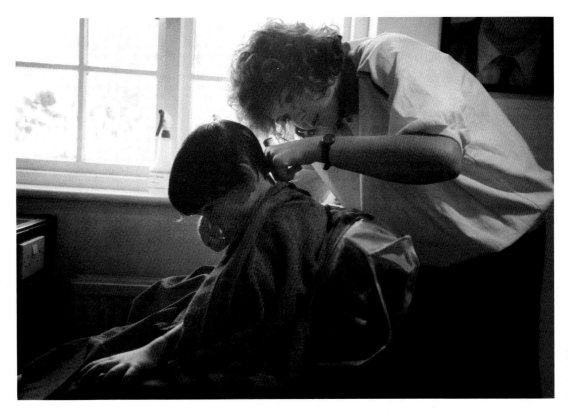

Kaye Bellman
DOMINIC AT THE HAIRDRESSERS
10.30am: Hemel Hempstead,
Hertfordshire

Mr F.W. Cooper
A BRIGHT NEW DAY
10.15am: Leigh-on-Sea, Essex

Mr G.J. Pile
'LUCKY' WITH HIS
ADOPTED MOTHER
10.30am: Haverfordwest,
Pembrokeshire

Eric Allday
OUTWARD BOUND
TRAINING COURSE
10.30am: Aberdovey, Gwynedd

Mr O.C. Neal
EVERYTHING STOPS
FOR THE HORSE
10.30am: Newmarket,
Cambridgeshire

Penny Thornton
THE TIMES, THEY ARE A-CHANGING
10.30am: Bramshott, Hampshire

Graham White
STUBBLE BURNING
10.30am: East Carlton,
Northamptonshire

Carol Sanders
I'LL HAVE A 99
10.30am: Bournemouth, Dorset

Bill Clarke
A POLICEMAN LENDS A HAND
10.30am: Offham, East Sussex

Dennis Jones
MY DOVES
10.35am: Burbage, Leicestershire

George Usher
HERIOT IN HEAVEN:
STICKLE GHYLL
10.30am: Langdale Valley,
Lake District

Graham Allen
FEN WORKERS' FIRE
10.35am: Wicken Fen,
Cambridgeshire

Alan D. Kennington
THATCHING, BRANSCOMBE
10.35am: Branscombe, East Devon

Rosalind Bramley
SPECTATOR, TOUR OF BRITAIN RACE
10.45am: Buxton, Derbyshire

Beryl Draisey
ROOF-TOP PHENOMENA!
10.40am: Headington, Oxford

Brian Speakman
ANNA AND KATIE
GO FRUIT-PICKING
11.00am: Wellington Heath,
Hertfordshire

David Owen
TEAMWORK
10.50am: Northolt, Middlesex

Margaret Andrews
MRS COOK AT THE HAIRDRESSERS
10.45am: Streatham Vale, London

Elizabeth Johnston
TWO GENERATIONS OF
BLACKSMITHS WORKING
11.00am: Dinas Cross, Dyfed

P.T. Warhurst
INQUISITIVE COWS
11.00am: East Stour, Dorset

Janet Keefe
LITTLE GIRLS AT THE PIANO
11.05am: Hanbury, Worcestershire

Patricia Crompton
HELPING OUT
11.00am: Biddulph, Stoke-on-Trent

Nigella Cowen
PEACE AND ISOLATION
11.05am: Alnwick to Rothbury Road,
Northumberland

Gareth Jennings
THE OLD STEEPLE VIEW
11.10am: Dundee, Tayside

Michael Nott
HOLIDAY FUN ON PAIGNTON PIER
11.05am: Paignton, Devon

G.B. Grandison
MOMENT OF CONTEMPLATION
11.00am: St John's Library, Worcester

R.W. Pike
KNOWN BY ALL – BUT FORGOTTEN
11.05am: Weymouth, Dorset

Barry Lockwood
THE KELLOGGS TOUR OF BRITAIN
11.10am: Buxton, Derbyshire

Overleaf:
Mr I.R. Flaherty
CHILDREN LAUGHING
11.10am: Ruxley Playgroup, London

Angela Tribe
'ELEVENSES', HELMSLEY MARKET
FISH STALL
11.10am: Helmsley Market,
North Yorkshire

Mr D. Waite
SAFELY GATHERED IN
11.05am: Chesham,
Buckinghamshire

D.J. Betts
WHEN DOES MY PARTY START?
11.10am: Godstrey, Cheshire

Katharine Mary Marr
A FINE DAY FOR DRYING
11.10am: Dorchester, Dorset

Deirdre Madgwick
UNDERTAKER'S WORKSHOP
11.15am: Grayshott, Hampshire

Andy Whale
UNDER LONDON
11.10am: Piccadilly Line,
London Underground

Revd Roland Stockley
CHILDREN PRAISING
AND HAVING FUN
11.15am: Criccieth, Gwynedd

Carol Conrich
WHOSE KNEE IS IT ANYWAY?
11.15am: Milton Keynes,
Buckinghamshire

Gina Holford
COFFEE TIME IN
THE SOCIAL CENTRE
11.15am: Loughton, Essex

Arthur Baker
THE FERRYMAN
11.20am: Southwold Harbour,
Suffolk

Barbara Bowie
SAM UNDER GRANDMA'S
CHRISTENING HAT
11.30am: Shoeburyness, Essex

Mrs P.E. Dawson
BATH BUN TIME – PUMP ROOM
11.15am: Bath, Avon

Mons Baker
AGELESS ENTERTAINMENT
11.30am: Southwold Beach, Suffolk

Graham L.N. Langworthy
THE 'MARY ROSE' PRESERVED
11.25am: Portsmouth, Hampshire

Dawn R. Lewis
WHERE'S MUM?
11.20am: Llantwit Major,
South Glamorgan

Mrs R. Hathaway
CHILD POSTING A LETTER
11.30am: Waterloo Station, London

Jean E. Lion
HOORAY, AND UP SHE RISES!
11.30am: Elie, Fifeshire

Maurice Burke
A BOWLS MATCH AT FELIXSTOWE
11.30am: Felixstowe, Suffolk

Mr C.R. Law
MAN ON A BENCH
11.30am: City Centre, Oxford

Linda Wearne
TRAIN DERAILMENT REPAIRS,
SNOWDON SUMMIT
11.30am: Mount Snowdon,
Gwynedd

Don Lawson
NORTHUMBRIAN NEATNESS
11.30am: B6318, close to
Hadrian's Wall, Northumberland

Cathy J. Pearson
THE WRECK-AGE
11.35am: Nuneaton, Warwickshire

Ken Dove
GRAFFITO ROLLER
11.30am: Wealdstone, Middlesex

Norman McBeath
AN IDEAL MORNING
11.40am: Cherwell Boat
House, Oxford

Mr R.C.F. Thompson
SPOILT FOR CHOICE
11.35am: Bracknell, Berkshire

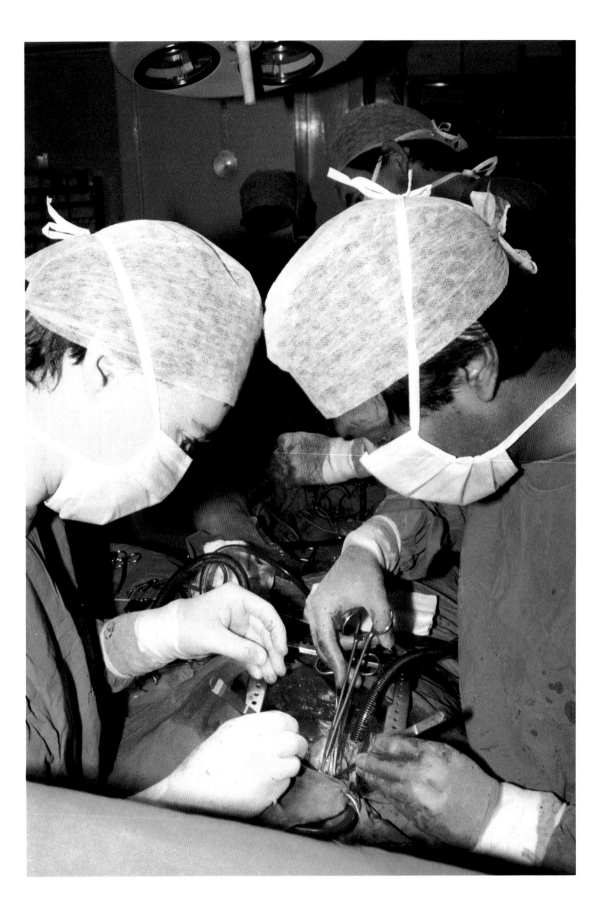

Ted van der Putt
OPEN HEART SURGERY AT THE
JOHN RADCLIFFE HOSPITAL
11.30am: Headington, Oxfordshire

Christine Hingley
GOING FISHING FROM STORNOWAY
11.40am: Stornoway, Isle of Lewis,
Outer Hebrides

O.B. Quinton
SHOPPING'S UNEXPECTED
HAZARDS!
11.45am: Henley-on-Thames,
Oxfordshire

A.J. Saunders
MOUNTIE GOES TO THE BANK
11.45am: Great Tower Street,
London

Gillian McCallum
THIS IS MY LIFE!
11.40am: Summertown,
Oxfordshire

E.V. Franklin
VICAR AND CHILD
11.40am: Lichfield, Staffordshire

Miss F.B. Mather
BOWLING THE HOOP
11.45am: Saltburn, Cleveland

Judith Curry
NOON NAP
12.00 noon: Plymouth, Devon

Clare Jenkins: Age 17
CHANGING BAIT
12.00 noon: River Medway,
Maidstone, Kent

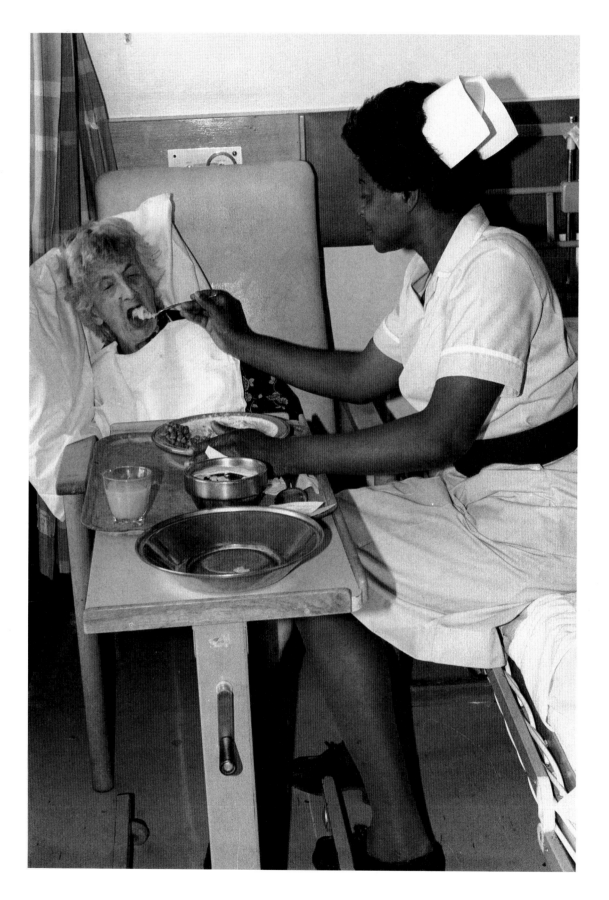

Mrs R. Glenister
I'M READY FOR THIS TODAY
12.00 noon: Walsgrave Hospital,
West Midlands

138

Peter Dazeley
DAVID SILVER BIRDIES
THE 18th GREEN
11.45am: 18th Green, The Berkshire

Jean I. Wiseman
HEADING TOWARDS LUNCH
12.00 noon: Bretforton,
Worcestershire

Sara Morgan
'PIP' SNAPPED CAT-NAPPING
12.00 noon: New Barnet,
Hertfordshire

Janice M. Gillespie
THE ELDERLY LADS OF ORKNEY
12.00 noon: Island of Orkney

G.S. Wells
THE VAGRANT'S B&B
12.15pm: Wood Hill, Northampton

Joan E. Sinclair
EVER STOICAL UNDER PRESSURE
12.00 noon: St James's Palace,
London

Philip Webb
EWBA WOMEN'S BOWLING
CHAMPIONSHIPS
12.00 noon: Leamington Spa,
Warwickshire

Janice Johns
SUNBATHING? WEYMOUTH BEACH
12.30pm: Weymouth, Dorset

Faith Price
COME ON OUT, FIDO
12.30pm: Wareham Quay, Dorset

Rachel Patterson
CAN WE BE GUARDSMEN TOO?
12.30pm: St James's Palace, London

Ben Austen
MY DAUGHTER EMILY
ON A TRAMPOLINE
12.00 noon: Swanage, Dorset

Peter James Atkinson
TENDING THE NETS
12.30pm: 'Seahouses' Harbour,
Northumberland

William McRoberts
HILL FARM
12.30pm: Ulster Folk Park,
Co Down

David Parker
AND THEN THERE WERE THREE!
12.30pm: London

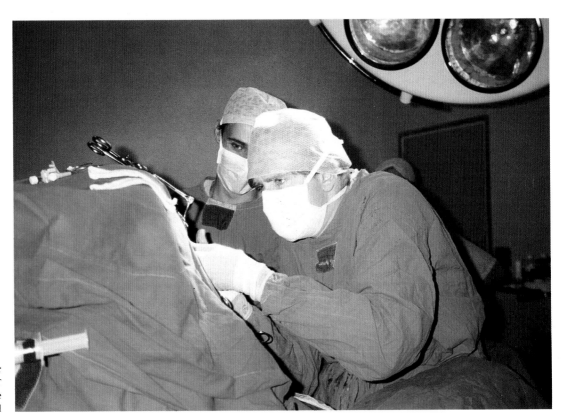

Dr Jean M. Millar
CANCER: THE FIGHT
12.30pm: Radcliffe
Infirmary, Oxford

Sheila Denahy
ONE DAY FOR DREAMING
12.00 noon: Southend-on-Sea, Essex

Val Valentini
GABRIELLA VALENTINI
12.30pm: Wimbledon, London

Ann Downing
DUCKS' DEVOTION
12.30pm: Woodbridge, Suffolk

Mrs G.I. McCombe
DAMP PICNIC AT CARTMEL
12.30pm: Cartmel Racecourse,
Cumbria

Denis Gerald Steel
KELLOGGS CYCLE RACE
12.30pm: Stoke, Staffordshire

George Usher
LANGDALE VALLEY FROM
HARRISON STICKLE
12.30pm: Langdale Valley,
Lake District

Pauline A. Spary
NEW LIFE IN THE MAKING
12.30pm: Letchworth, Hertfordshire

Carol Steele
COCKINGTON VILLAGE
12.30pm: Cockington, Devon

Jean Davies
STREET ENTERTAINER
12.40pm: City Centre, Cardiff

Joseph Lynch
ENJOYING LIFE'S LITTLE LUXURIES
12.30pm: Princes Street, Edinburgh

Marion Sharp
POPPIES IN A CORNFIELD
12.30pm: Upper Winchendon,
Buckinghamshire

Sheila Denahy
LOW TIDE
12.35pm: Southend-on-Sea, Essex

Stephanie Wilson
A GIRL'S BEST FRIEND
12.45pm: Liss, Hampshire

Hylda C. Peart
COMMUNICATION CORNER
12.45pm: Thornbury, Avon

Joyce Sherburn
JOB SEARCH 80s STYLE
12.50pm: Exeter, Devon

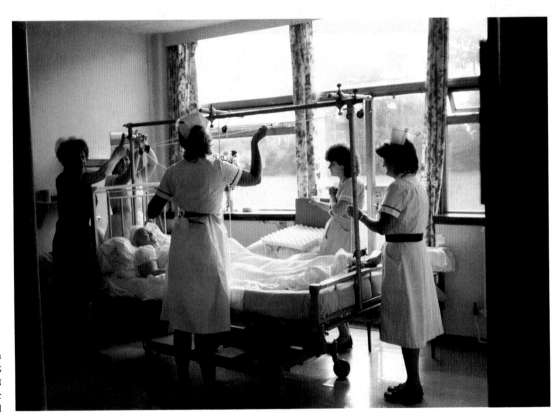

Margaret Mary Ogden
WARD STAFF ADJUSTING
PATIENT'S TRACTION
12.45pm: Nuffield Orthopaedic
Centre, Oxford

Chris Gilbert
BREAK FROM WORK
12.45pm: Covent Garden, London

Simon C. Polley
A BROKEN-DOWN
BREAKDOWN TRUCK
12.45pm: Theydon Bois, Essex

Ralph Baker
BUILDERS AT LUNCHTIME
12.45pm: Maidenhead, Berkshire

R.H. Chadwick
A LUNCHTIME BREAK
12.55pm: Langley Park, Berkshire

Mrs M.M. Worthington
HOORAY! DAD PASSED HIS TEST
12.50pm: Stevenage, Hertfordshire

Mr W.S. Giles
A FRIENDLY CHAT VIA 'BUZBY'
12.40pm: Southampton, Hampshire

Robert W. White
BUSKER IN EASTGATE STREET
1.00pm: City Centre, Chester

Leonard A.W. Rentmore
ON GUARD AT WINDSOR CASTLE
1.00pm: Windsor, Berkshire

Kevin O'Connor
CONCRETE GANG
1.00pm: Kingston Upon Thames,
Surrey

Elaine Hoare
CLASSICAL PAVEMENT ARTIST
1.00pm: Bath, Avon

Chris Gilbert
BUSKING IN COVENT GARDEN
1.00pm: Covent Garden, London

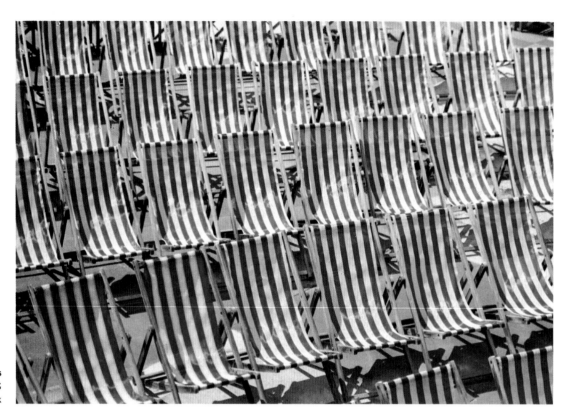

Brian A. Brookes
READY AND WAITING
1.00pm: Eastbourne, Sussex

Harry Baron
DERELICT MAN IN SHADE
1.00pm: Sheffield, South Yorkshire

G.A. Dingley
FAMILY JOY
1.00pm: Bushey, Hertfordshire

Carol Margaret Warbrick
LORD OF ALL I SURVEY!
1.39pm: Lichfield, Staffordshire

Mrs M.M. Bailey
VIEW FROM ON HIGH
1.00pm: Great St Mary's Tower,
Cambridge

David Coan
STREET MUSICIANS AND SHOPPERS
1.10pm: City Centre, Manchester

James Manson Dallas
HANDS UP! THE EDINBURGH
FESTIVAL
1.00pm: Mound Square, Edinburgh

Robin Wilkieson
INTER-TIDAL OYSTER
FARMERS AT WORK
1.00pm: West Loch, Tarbert, Argyll

Mrs M.M. Bailey
THE 'EAGLE', FRIDAY LUNCHTIME
1.15pm: Benet Street, Cambridge

Gordon W. Taylor
SUMMER BARGAIN HUNTERS
1.15pm: High Town, Hereford

Jean Smithson
CHILDREN DRINKING
AT THE FOUNTAIN
1.30pm: The Rye, High Wycombe,
Buckinghamshire

Andrew Hastie
'LINDA' AT BLAENAU
FFESTINIOG STATION
1.30pm: Blaenau Ffestiniog,
Gwynedd

Gary Thomas
COLOURFUL PROMOTION
1.00pm: City Centre, Derby

Mr P.J. Tomlinson
'AYBEE' MAINTAINING
BRITAIN'S HERITAGE
1.22pm: Grafton Regis,
Northamptonshire

Norman McBeath
PARKED UP AT THE PARK
1.30pm: Oxford

Jocelyn R. Hunt
FASCINATING BEHAVIOUR
1.30pm: Covent Garden, London

Alistair Linford
A FAMILY OUTING
1.30pm: Plymouth Ho, Devon

Patrine Miller
OUR ROYAL HERITAGE
2.00pm: Hampton Court, Surrey

Iris Burford
FINISHING TOUCH
1.30pm: Winchester, Hampshire

Glenys Thornton
A DAY AT THE SEASIDE
1.30pm: Clacton-on-Sea, Essex

Findlay Rankin
NEWLY PROMOTED SERGEANTS
2.00pm: Glasgow, Strathclyde

Margaret Coling
TWO'S DAY FOR LIFE
2.00pm: Ryde, Isle of Wight

Peter M. Upton
WELDING EXHAUST SYSTEMS
2.00pm: Oxford

Mrs L.E. Jensen
IT'S JUST NOT CRICKET!
2.00pm: Bryanston, Blandford,
Dorset

Stephen Chape
GRAND-DAUGHTER LAURA TYLER
AND FRIENDS
2.00pm: Washington, Tyne & Wear

John Howard
LONELY PLOUGHMAN ON
LINCOLNSHIRE WOLDS
2.00pm: Kirmond le Mire,
Lincolnshire

John Robertson
A SINGLE PROTEST FOR PEACE
2.00pm: Molesworth,
Cambridgeshire

Gareth Watkins
IMRAN KHAN SIGNS AUTOGRAPHS
2.00pm: Cheam, Surrey

William Ashmore
WE AIM TO CONQUER CANCER
2.00pm: Kensington Palace
Gardens, London

Henry William Nicholson
WHAT TROLLEY?
2.00pm: Bletchley, Buckinghamshire

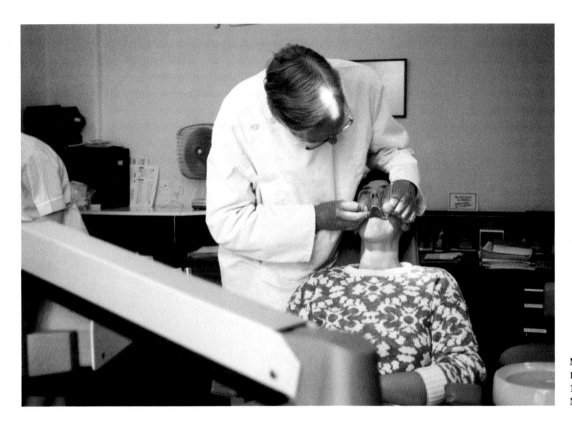

Maureen F. Pattinson
ROUTINE DENTAL CARE
1.50pm: South Molton,
North Devon

Horace Anderson
ONE WAY TO ENJOY RETIREMENT
1.45pm: Pateley Bridge, Yorkshire

Mrs J.B. Kingscott
IS ANYBODY THERE?
1.45pm: Fife, Scotland

I invariably find a deep joy in being in my home where I have known so much love and where I have had endless proof of God's caring for us in time of stress and difficulty. To be at home surrounded by mementos reminding me of other happy days gives me occasion to count my blessings. When I think of those who are not as fortunate as I have been and all those who are still struggling against cancer I thank God for the mercies I have known. So in sharing this picture with readers I am sharing something of the depth of feeling I have for all who are fighting against the dread disease.
Thank God for the carers.

LORD TONYPANDY

The
AFTERNOON

2.00-6.00

On August 14th, my delight in the possibility of being part of this wonderful book soon gave way to despair. My aim was to photograph the family plus assorted livestock looking animated on our little bridge and call it a Bridge Party. Alas, they all shoved off to the pub at lunchtime where, because someone's horse had won a cup, it was champagne on the house. When they finally trooped home at 3.45 the sun had gone, and by the time I'd assembled five cats on the bridge, my husband, my daughter and her friend and both dogs had sobered up and had great difficulty smiling. My son, emulating the sun, vanished too, and at the first camera-click the cats bolted never to return. The experience has given me an even deeper respect for all professional and amateur photographers.

JILLY COOPER

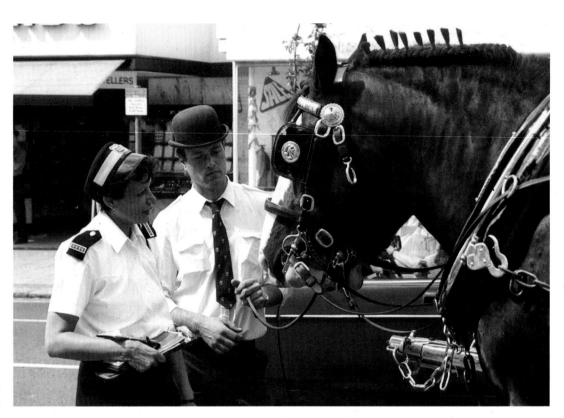

John Billingham
A VEHICLE OR A PET?
2.15pm: Ealing Broadway, London

John Wellesley
PAINTING ON A
SUNLIT AFTERNOON
3.30pm: Bampton, Oxfordshire

Robert John Fraser
THE HAND OF FRIENDSHIP
2.28pm: Bosherston, Pembrokeshire

Norman McBeath
WORKING IT OUT
2.15pm: Oxford

Stephen Anthony Ellis
CHILD WITH GRANDFATHER
AT THE BEACH
2.30pm: Paignton, South Devon

Enid L. Prater
THE MAJESTIC SEA
2.30pm: Scarborough,
North Yorkshire

Steve Barney
PADDLING PALS – STUART
AND WILLIAM SMITH
2.30pm: Corby, Northamptonshire

Angela Towell: Age 15
HORSE CROSSING FORD
IN WYCOLLER
2.30pm: Wycoller, Lancashire

Zbigniew Stankiewicz
PILOT AND SON
2.30pm: RAF Odiham, Hampshire

Miss D. Gregory
FARRIER AT WORK
2.40pm: Maidenhead, Berkshire

Kathleen Woodcock
OVER 60s KEEP FIT CLASS
2.42pm: Scarborough,
North Yorkshire

Christopher Cotton
ASSYNT HIGHLAND GAMES
3.00pm: Lochinver, Highlands

Brian Highley
ICE CREAM – MUM SCREAMS!
3.00pm: Exmouth, Devon

Kathleen Sargent
A GLIMPSE OF SUMMER SUNSHINE
3.00pm: Dent, Cumbria

M.D. Rice-Oxley
SHOE SIESTA
3.00pm: Teddington, Middlesex

P. Willis
OLD GABLES
3.00pm: Bitterley, Shropshire

Mr D. Jenkins
SNOWDON MOUNTAIN RAILWAY
3.00pm: Mount Snowdon,
Gwynedd

Cyril Harrison
FEEDING TIME
3.00pm: Buxton, Derbyshire

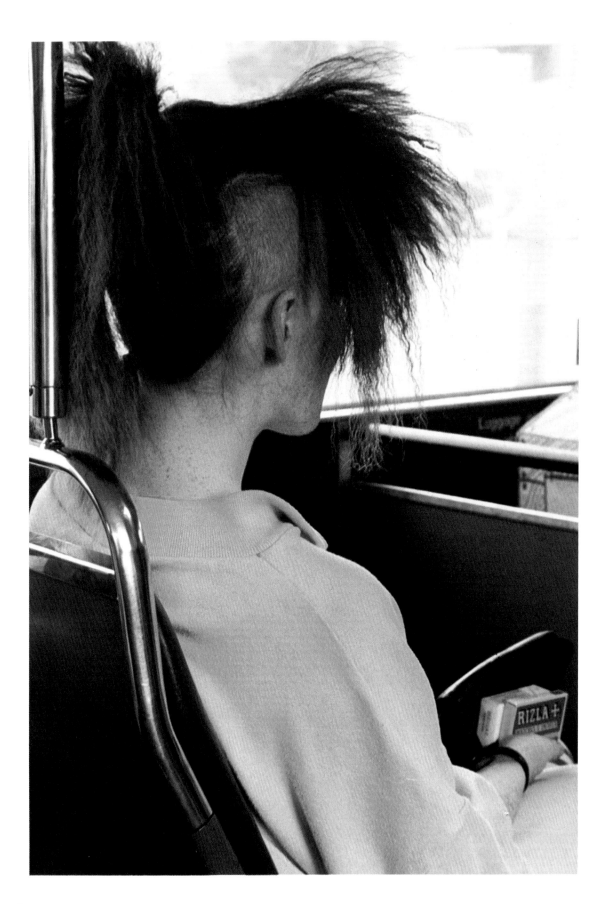

Mr B. Rullis
JOURNEY IN THE PINK
3.15pm: Leeds, West Yorkshire

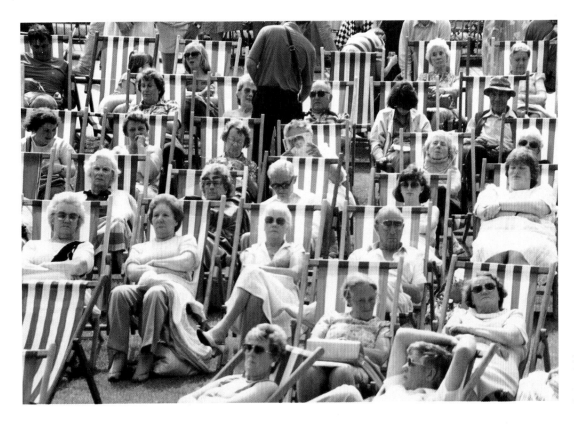

Martin Best
MILITARY BAND CONCERT
AUDIENCE
3.30pm: Bournemouth, Dorset

Roland James Boon
KATIE, HEADING FOR THE SHORE!
3.25pm: Weymouth, Dorset

Robert John Fraser
A PAIR OF BEACH BUMS
3.05pm: Broadhaven Beach,
Pembrokeshire

Glenn Taylor
CHIPS AT THE FUN FAIR
3.30pm: Hunstanton, Norfolk

Liz Felgate
LIA AND FFION BY THE SEA
3.30pm: Ynyslas Barth, Dyfed

Joseph Lynch
A 'PUNK' PIPER
3.30pm: Princes Street, Edinburgh

Jennifer Anne Denning
SHAVING AND SHARING
3.30pm: City Centre, Cardiff

Paul Dawson
ANOTHER DAY'S NEWS
3.30pm: Strand Palace Hotel,
London

Ronald Arthur Harvey
IF ONLY IT WAS SNOW
3.30pm: Swadlincote Ski Slope,
Derbyshire

Cameron John Watters
LET'S SEE WHAT'S UP HERE
3.30pm: Sunderland, Tyne & Wear

Susan M. Jones
GRUBBY HUBBY
3.30pm: Little Sutton, Cheshire

Sidney Lennie
KNEELING MONK AT
NORTON PRIORY
3.55pm: Runcorn, Cheshire

Sally Belinda Carter
HIGH STREET SHOPPER
3.30pm: Ballards Lane, London

Marjorie Thacker
BARLOW WELL-DRESSING
3.55pm: Barlow, Derbyshire

Eric Coppock
THE BRIDE'S DAY
4.00pm: Beaconsfield,
Buckinghamshire

A. Walters
A HAIR-RAISING EXPERIENCE
4.00pm: Science Museum, London

Gilbert Murray
PUNTING ON THE CAM
4.00pm: Cambridge

Mrs E.I. Wood
BEACH GAMES
4.00pm: Whitby, North Yorkshire

Nicola Watts
EMILY WATTS ON HER TRACTOR
4.00pm: Bury St Edmunds, Suffolk

Patricia Aithie
MINE DETECTION
4.00pm: Cardiff Castle

Mr J.D. Cox
HILLSIDE HARVESTING
4.00pm: Cerne Valley, Dorset

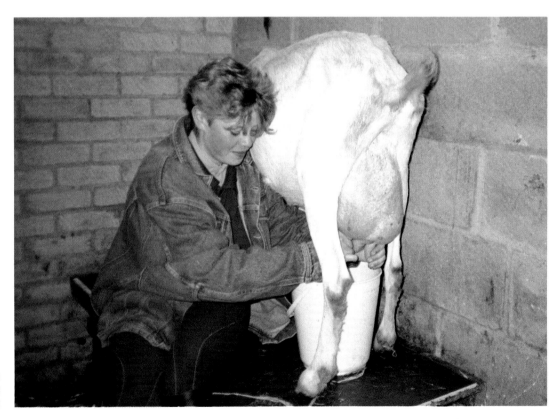

Dawn Suzanne Fairhurst: Age 10
MILKING TIME
4.00pm: Llanfairfechan, Gwynedd

Jennifer M. Prince-McPherson
INTERESTED SPECTATORS!
4.00pm: Hartley Wintney,
Hampshire

Steve Rockall
TIGHT INTO THE CHICANE
4.15pm: Silverstone Racing Circuit,
Northamptonshire

Mary Harrison
GOLFERS BELOW
ST ENODOC CHURCH
4.00pm: Bray Hill, Cornwall

Patricia Aithie
THE SENIOR SERVICE
– CARDIFF TATTOO
4.10pm: Cardiff Castle

Paul Brodie
THE DESCENT
3.30pm: Poole, Dorset

Robert David Briars
THE END OF THE LINE
4.15pm: Scrap Yard, Leicester

Jean Kendall
COLLECTING COWS FOR
EVENING MILKING
4.30pm: Crawcrook, Tyne & Wear

Coila Clyne
OH, I WAS THIRSTY
4.30pm: High
Wogan Winne

Judy Price
PLAYTIME IN BRIGHT COLOURS
4.30pm: Bristol, Avon

Martin Lloyd-Elliott
THE BLUES MAN: 'TAKE FIVE'
4.30pm: Leicester Square, London

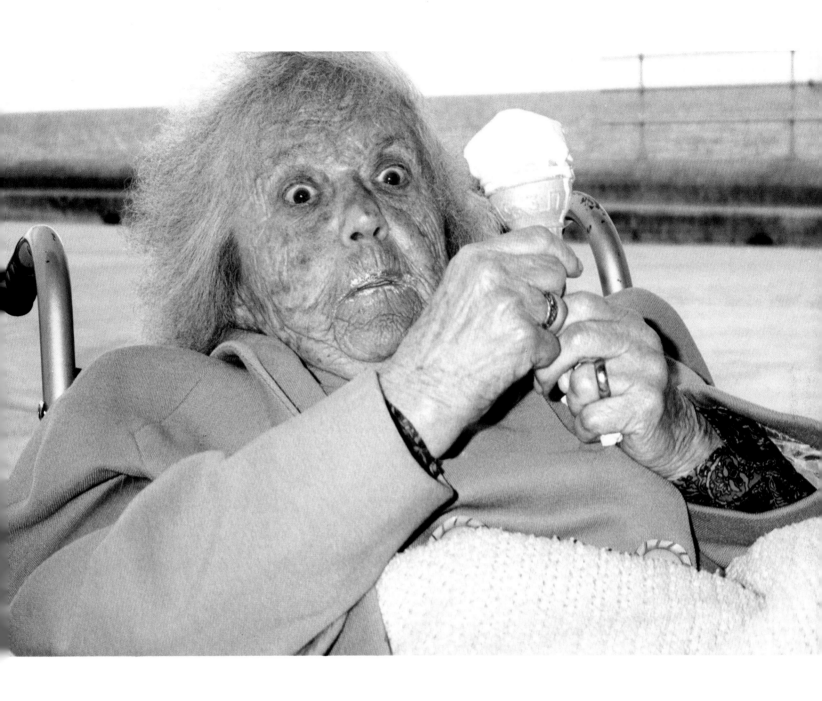

Michael Pilkington
SURPRISE TREAT FOR GRAN
4.40pm: Blackpool, Lancashire

Katherine Ann Howell
EVENING STROLL
5.00pm: Bathley, Newark-on-Trent

Mr J.K. Cuthbertson
A SLIDE OF HAPPINESS
6.00pm: Newton Stewart, Galloway

Richard Aylward
SUNSET ON WINDERMERE
5.00pm: The Ferry,
Lake Windermere

Mary Harrison
RED SAILS
5.05pm: Camel Estuary, Cornwall

Nigel Lea-Jones
FLOWER GIRLS
5.20pm: Covent Garden, London

Ian Alexander Van der Ende
A BEE-KEEPER AT WORK
5.30pm: Woodbridge, Suffolk

Doreen May Lording
LIFE EVERLASTING
6.00pm: Garstang, Lancashire

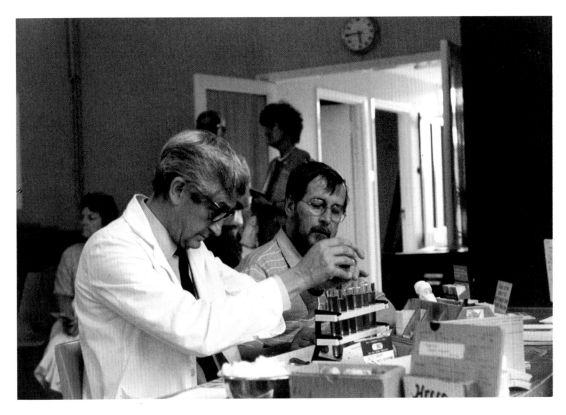

John Freeman
THE BLOOD DONOR
5.45pm: Downend, Bristol, Avon

Gilbert Murray
WOMEN RUNNERS
6.00pm: Crystal Palace, London

Joanna Rice
EARLY-EVENING SUN
6.00pm: Bude, North Cornwall

E.A. McQuillan
PREPARING FOR AN EVENING OUT
6.00pm: Tower Hamlets, London

Peter Eric Holt
RED DEVIL ON TARGET
6.00pm: Bristol, Avon

'You're on next!'... I took this photograph of Gloria Hunniford shortly after arriving at Broadcasting House where I was to be a guest on her radio programme. I remember being very impressed by how relaxed she was on the air, as the picture shows. It had already been a very busy day since I had spent the morning in a recording studio in North London where I was narrating Charles Dickens' *A Christmas Carol*. I just had time for a quick plate of sandwiches before being whisked off to the BBC, camera at the ready.

ALED JONES

The
EVENING

6.00-12.00

This may seem to the imperceptive and less discerning to be just another photo
of the cognoscenti and high livers that frequent *Wogan* on any Monday,
Wednesday or Friday you may care to mention. Not so, my littles. This photo
represents nothing less than a major effort to get up there with Parkinson,
Snowdon, Bailey and Donovan. Why should they have all the plum jobs, the
most exotic locations, the best-looking bimbos, while I am stuck here in
Shepherd's Bush with the bag ladies? Fair do's, and I didn't even have
a lens hood...

TERRY WOGAN

Colin MacPherson
HARVESTING ON THE
SUSSEX DOWNS
6.15pm: Near Ditchling Beacon,
Sussex

J.E.N. Davey
POST OFFICE STORES, BARDFIELD
6.15pm: Great Bardfield, Essex

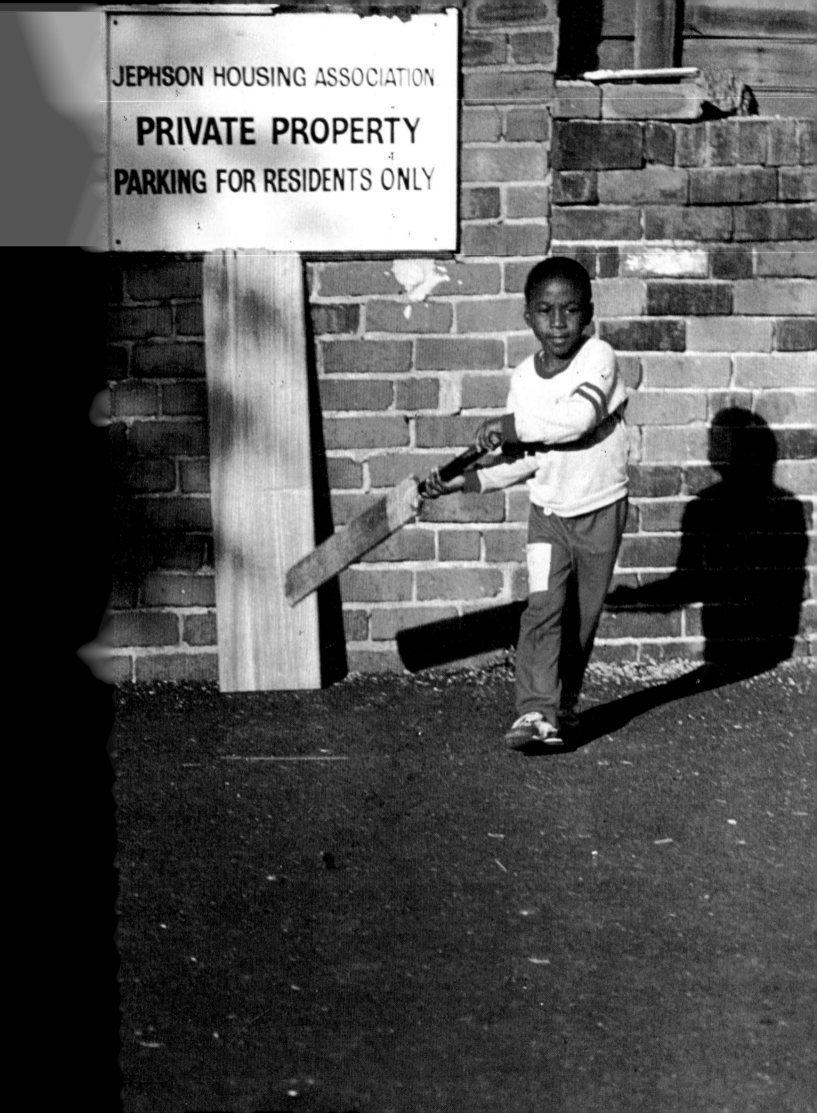

Mandy Jane Brooks
PASTEL REFLECTIONS
6.15pm: The River Cam, Cambridge

E. Aldred
YOUNG CHAMPS
6.15pm: London

Brian William Gamston
NEVER TOO YOUNG TO LEARN
6.30pm: Dudley, West Midlands

Garry Bosworth
FRIENDS FOR LIFE
6.30pm: Bracebridge Heath, Lincoln

Richard Webb
REG BATCHELOR AT WORK
6.45pm: Helmdon,
Northamptonshire

Tom Craig
SMALL BUSINESSMEN
6.30pm: Wickford, Essex

Dominic Cragoe
BEASTIE BOYS VW BADGE MANIA
7.00pm: Reading, Berkshire

John Ainsworth
CHILDHOOD INNOCENCE
7.00pm: St Leonards on Sea,
East Sussex

Derek Hayes
RISKING A QUICK SINGLE
6.30pm: Stevenage, Hertfordshire

Mrs H.M. Wood
MARE AND FOAL
7.00pm: Thornhill, Dewsbury,
West Yorkshire

Mr W.L. Coulter
BEACHED SHIP
7.00pm: Blyth, Northumberland

Rita Dawson
YOUTHFUL SCENE FOR
HOPEFUL FUTURE
7.15pm: Romford, Essex

Valerie Johns
THE HARVEST IS OVER
7.00pm: Gainsborough,
Lincolnshire

Miss M.K. Padgett
CONTRASTING EVENING LIGHT
7.00pm: Bude, North Cornwall

Alan Winn
PHONIN'
7.00pm: Glasgow Central Station

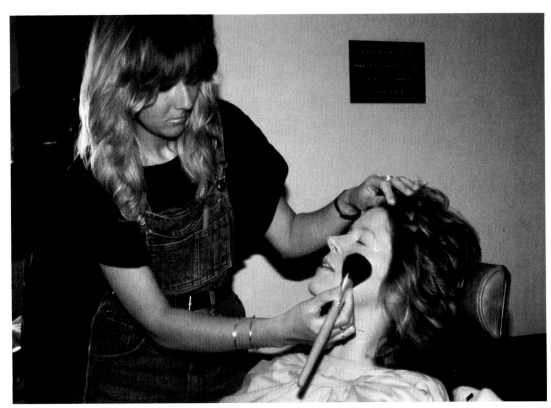

Anthony Holland
JULIA SOMMERVILLE'S
LAST 9 O'CLOCK NEWS
7.00pm: BBC TV Centre, London

Yvonne Lloyd-Jones
THAT BIT'S FOR ME!
7.00pm: Abersoch, Gwynedd

Robert Farrow
A CRITICAL VIEW
7.00pm: Thorpe Bay, Essex

Francis H. Paton
THE MILK OF HUMAN KINDNESS
7.00pm: Danby Wiske,
North Yorkshire

Claire Hodson
WHOSE BATH IS THIS ANYWAY?
7.20pm: Westminster, London

Jane Wedmore
LAST TRIP? THEN A BEER...
7.30pm: Cambridge

Mr L. Croucher
TERRY'S OVERJOYED
WITH POLAROID
7.30pm: TV screen, London

Pat Maycroft
CHILDREN'S SPORTS AT
ALDBROUGH FEAST
7.10pm: Richmond,
North Yorkshire

E. Brenda Linley
YOUTHFUL CURIOSITY
7.30pm: Stainburn, North Yorkshire

Mr R.W. Sands
A SWALLOW FEEDING ITS YOUNG
7.30pm: Boston, Lincolnshire

Tom Langlands
FISHING NETS ON THE SOLWAY
7.35pm: Solway Firth, Powfoot

Jane Hardwick
EVENING POPPIES
7.30pm: Chesterfield, Derbyshire

Raymond V. Williams
BABES IN THE WOOD
7.30pm: Wraxall, Avon

Victoria Randolph: Age 15
HARVEST SUN
7.30pm: Binfield, Berkshire

Mrs D. Bunker
I'M NOT DOING ANY MORE!
7.30pm: Arnold, Nottinghamshire

K.R. Carter
EVENING ON THE RIVER ORWELL
8.15pm: Woolverstone Marina,
Suffolk

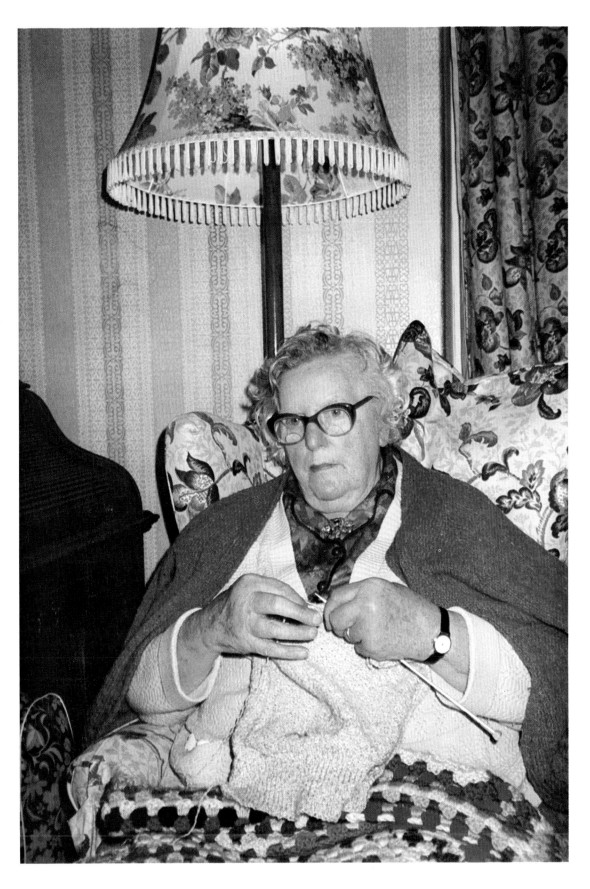

Miss G.G. Sharman
MOTHER KNITTING
7.30pm: Redcar, Cleveland

David Moxham
SUNSET – STAMSHAW FORESHORE
9.00pm: Stamshaw, Portsmouth,
Hampshire

John Adams
THE SPLENDOUR OF
THE UNDERWORLD
8.00pm: Ogof Capel, Gwent

Paul A. Cooper
GIPSY CHILDREN AMONGST
INDUSTRIAL RUBBISH
8.05pm: Industrial Site, York

Dr A.P.S. Kimberley
OSCAR SHUMSKY AT THE PROMS
8.15pm: Royal Albert Hall, London

Brian Hall
A FISHERMAN'S SUNSET
8.00pm: Grafham Water,
Cambridgeshire

Christopher Jones
CRICCIETH CASTLE
FROM BLACK ROCK
8.00pm: Black Rock Sands,
North Wales

Yvonne Brothers
SHOOTING THE RAPIDS
8.00pm: Whitesands, Dumfries

Angela Helen Buckley
BRITISH CATERING FOR
MADONNA'S FANS
8.00pm: Leeds, West Yorkshire

Susan Westwood
SWEET DREAMS
8.15pm: Radcliffe-on-Trent,
Nottinghamshire

Tony Smith
SUNSET OVER GOONHILLY
8.16pm: Goonhilly Downs,
Cornwall

Peter Upton
CATCH THE WIND
8.30pm: Brill Common,
Buckinghamshire

Manus R. McGinty
HOME FIRES BURNING
8.30pm: Kirkinch, Tayside

Joan Littler
EVENING REFLECTIONS
OF INDUSTRY
8.30pm: Frodsham, Cheshire

John F. Bradley
RIVER FOYLE, DERRY
10.00pm: Culmore Point,
near Derry City

Doris Stubbs
FISHERMEN AT SUNSET
8.45pm: Combe Martin,
North Devon

June Margaret Wiltshire
EVENING TRANQUILLITY
8.30pm: Backwell Pond,
Bristol, Avon

Richard W.A. Dumville
NORTH–SOUTH HIGHWAY
8.30pm: M1 Junction 30,
Barlborough, Derbyshire

Sheila Wooton
THE BOOK OF REVELATIONS
9.00pm: A Safe House,
High Wycombe, Buckinghamshire

Vicki Mould
SUNSET ANGLING, CLAYPOOL
8.50pm: Christchurch, Dorset

Jeremy Chaplin
A VIEW TO A THRILL
9.00pm: Aylesbury,
Buckinghamshire

Nicholas Charles Williams
PULTENEY BRIDGE AT NIGHT
9.30pm: Bath, Avon

Robert Graeme Newall
REFLECT UPON A SPECIAL DAY
9.00pm: Cullercoats Harbour,
Tyne & Wear

Tracey Byard
THE WHEEL OF FUN!
9.00pm: Aylesbury,
Buckinghamshire

Mrs S.M. Skingle
CAN YOU COUNT MY CLAWS?
10.00pm: Stansted, Essex

Mrs V. Moorhouse
WELCOME VISITORS
9.35pm: Rylstone, North Yorkshire

Josephine Nowlan
SUNSET, CLOUDS,
YOUNG COUPLE, SEA
10.30pm: The Western Highlands

Stephen Murray
FLAMING WASTE OF
GOOD BRANDY!
9.45pm: Kings Lynn, Norfolk

Overleaf:
Caroline Harrhy
CAERPHILLY CASTLE BY NIGHT
10.30pm: Caerphilly,
Mid Glamorgan

Norman Shankland
BACKWATER
10.48pm: Wishaw, Lanarkshire

Heather M. Chandler
HOME COMPUTER – LATE
NIGHT ADDICTION
10.30pm: Ashby-de-la-Zouch,
Leicestershire

James Duncan Saul
BIRMINGHAM – ONE NIGHT
FOR LIFE
10.30pm: City Centre, Birmingham

John Londei
IN THE LIMELIGHT
11.00pm: Limelight Nightclub,
London

R. Chalmers
IS IT YOUR ROUND?
11.30pm: Wilmslow, Cheshire

Mrs M.P. Merison
DEAR PRUDENCE
12.00 midnight: Narborough,
Leicestershire

David Smith
THE END OF ONE DAY
11.55pm: Cherry Garden Pier,
London

Sylvia Williams
MIDNIGHT FEAST
(WITH GORDON THE GOFER)
11.55pm: Fenwick, Ayrshire

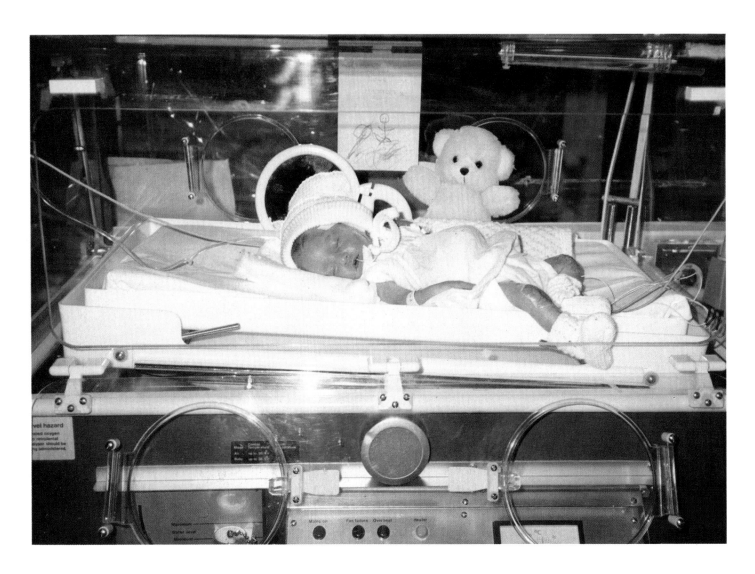

Henriette Hayden
SARAH PHELPS
12.00 midnight: Musgrove Park
Hospital, Taunton, Somerset
(Sarah's mother died of cancer
24 hours after the birth)

This photograph was taken on what was a fairly ordinary day for me. I had just left my management office and took the picture because it captures most things that are typical of London: the Thames, Battersea Bridge, boats and houseboats, traffic jams, black cabs, high-rise buildings. The reason the picture is in black and white is because it was a dull, grey day – also typical of London!

MIDGE URE

As Seen by the Press

Ros Drinkwater
The Times
THE 62,848th BACK PAGE OF
THE TIMES (Editor: Charles Wilson)
**Winner of "The SupaSnaps Press
Photographer of the Day" trophy**

Bobby Davro
The Daily Star
RUSS ABBOTT

Ted Blackburn
The Daily Mail
TOUCHDOWN

Richard Reed
The Sun
THE LONG AND SHORT OF IT

Barry Gomer
The Daily Express
MADONNA AND HER MINDERS

Don McPhee
The Guardian
BIG-TOP BAPTISM

Herbie Knott
The Independent
CHASING THE STEAM

The Pilot: Charlie Shea-Simonds, Chairman of the
Royal Aero Club with his rebuilt Tiger Moth
(photo: Herbie Knott)

The Driver: Tom Turner, shed foreman of the
Mid-Hants Railway
(photo: Herbie Knott)

As Seen Through Other Well Known Eyes

Michael Crawford (self-portrait taken while being made-up for a performance of *Phantom of the Opera*)

Jane Bown

Terence Donovan

Dick Jones

Terry O'Neill

Linda McCartney

Terry Jones

Heather Angel

Daley Thompson

Patrick Lichfield

Gene Nocon

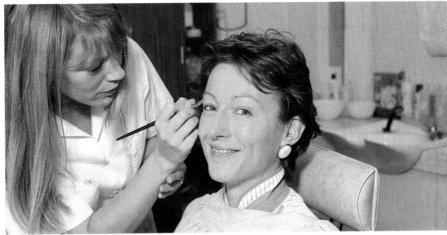

Pamela Armstrong

John Francome

Paul Daniels

Ronnie Barker

POSTSCRIPT

"I'm sorry – I had no film in my camera, but this
photograph was taken on August 14th 1915.
It shows my two big sisters who have now
died of cancer."

G.M. HOLLAND
Ealing, London

Afterword

Cancer is a terrible disease that can affect any one of us at any time. Despite great advances in the treatment and care of people with cancer and successes in cancer research, one in three people in this country still suffer from the disease, many of whom will not survive.

It was against this background that Gareth Pyne-James first approached me in November 1986 with his ideas for a massive fund-raising project – SEARCH 88. At the time, the whole scheme seemed somewhat fantastic, but within that year SEARCH 88 became very much a reality.

SEARCH 88 is the largest co-ordinated fund-raising initiative against cancer ever seen in this country. It has the support of the Joint British Cancer Charities, who will be the major beneficiaries of the SEARCH 88 Cancer Trust, alongside many other smaller cancer charities in this country whom we hope to be able to help.

Funds for the SEARCH 88 Cancer Trust will be raised through a series of major public events like *One Day for Life*, which will take place throughout 1988, when we will be urging everyone to become involved in the campaign.

One Day for Life has been a tremendous success, and certainly captured the imagination of the British public. Apart from the considerable amounts of money raised, I feel that this magnificent book is proof of what SEARCH 88 can and will achieve in the future.

There are numerous people to thank for making SEARCH 88 a success.

Firstly Gareth, without whose idea, enthusiasm, dedication and plain hard work SEARCH 88 would never have happened. He is a man with the inspiration to dream up such a project, and the determination to see it come to fruition.

Also the team at SEARCH 88, comprising Beverley Bailey, Beatle Langrishe, Lucinda Pugh and Christopher English, who have all worked to make Gareth's dream a reality.

The basic philosophy behind SEARCH 88 is that all public donations are passed entirely into the SEARCH 88 Cancer Trust without any deductions for administrative or other costs. This could not be done without the generous support of the major sponsors: Bantam Press, Barclays Bank plc, Fuji Film, Hertz Europe Ltd and SupaSnaps Ltd. Our grateful thanks go to these our main sponsors, as well as the ever-growing membership of the SEARCH 88 Supporters Club.

Thanks also go to the individuals and companies who have helped us in numerous ways. Our Vice-Presidents, Trustees and professional advisers have given us invaluable support.

There are two individuals who merit special thanks. Firstly, Her Royal Highness The Duchess of York who, as Patron of the SEARCH 88 Cancer Trust, has devoted much of her time to the cause, for which we are very grateful. Secondly, Clive Jermain – a young man suffering from spinal cancer, who, through his work for SEARCH 88 and his courage and resilience, has been an inspiration to us all.

Lastly, and most importantly, the contribution and support of the British public has been a vital ingredient in the success of *One Day for Life*. This is your book, created by you, for you, and one which I hope will be a lasting record of Britain on one very special day. Thank you.

RICHARD HAMBRO
President of the SEARCH 88 Cancer Trust

Supporters

Our grateful thanks to the following companies, and their staff, without whose physical and financial contributions SEARCH 88 would not exist.

They are:

A.D. Consultants
Airship Industries (UK) Limited
David Anthony Pharmaceuticals
British Broadcasting Corporation
Bronica (UK) Limited
Burson–Marsteller
Collett, Dickenson, Pearce and Partners Limited Advertising
Collett, Dickenson, Pearce – Network Limited
Colorgraphic Printers Limited
Coutts & Company
Cranwell Stationers
Daiwa Europe Limited
S. Daniels plc
EMI Records (UK) Limited
Farrer & Company
Fine Art Developments plc
Glass Glover Group plc
J.O. Hambro & Company Limited
Hambros plc
HFC Trust & Savings Limited
Kingfisher Wallcoverings
The Lynton Group
Arthur Maiden Limited
More O'Ferrall Adshel
Nabisco Group Limited
Nassus Print and Design
Network Distribution Limited
Olympus Optic Company (UK) Limited
Peat, Marwick, McLintock
PHM Integrated Direct Marketing
Helena Rubinstein Limited
Spark Sponsorship Company Limited
Standard Chartered plc
John Taylor International
Thames Television plc
TNT Roadfreight
Tokina (UK) Limited
Waterford-Aynsley (UK) Limited
Yorkshire Bank plc

And with grateful thanks and appreciation to the booksellers of the United Kingdom – large and small alike – who have supported *One Day for Life* so magnificently, and without whose help the royalty contributions from the sale of this book would not have been possible.

Index

This book was designed by A.D. Consultants, London.
Art Director: Bob Searles. **Book Designer:** Antony Johnson. **Design Team:** Charles Campbell, Bernhard Chandler, Andy Clements (typesetting), Stuart Dickinson, Nick Hockley, Nick Kaminsky, Gary Kemp, Alan Stratford. **Photographic printers:** Brian Fay, Peter Ewusi-Aikens, Dave McCarthy, Simon De Senneville.

My One Day for Life
Clive Jermain

On August 14th it was a wonderful feeling to think that people the length and breadth of Britain were going out and taking a photo, capturing a unique day and making their own special contribution in the fight against what is a terrible disease (I talk from experience).

Personally, too, the day was very special to me. My photo for the day was of important people in my life and of all my friends at the BBC who have helped me in achieving my goals and ambitions in TV terms, which has been the most important thing in my life, firstly with the play and now with presenting. Also present was someone who has been very special in my life recently, Gareth Pyne-James, who has put in all the work and effort to set up SEARCH 88, which has enabled me to campaign for better cancer care today as well as research into a cure for tomorrow.

Photography has always been very important to me in immortalising my life and taking my photo today of all my friends outside BBC TV Centre has immortalised a very special day and is also my way of saying 'thank you' to them all.

The Hon. Angus Ogilvy
A CHAMPAGNE DAY
11.05am: BBC TV Centre, London